TIGER

Dylanna Press

Copyright © 2022 by Dylanna Press
Author: Tyler Grady

All rights reserved. No part of this publication may be reproduced, stored in a retrieval system, or transmitted by any means, including electronic, mechanical, photocopying, or otherwise, without prior written permission of the publisher.

Although the publisher has taken all reasonable care in the preparation of this book, we make no warranty about the accuracy or completeness of its content and, to the maximum extent permitted, disclaim all liability arising from its use.

Trademarks: Dylanna Press is a registered trademark of Dylanna Publishing, Inc. and may not be used without written permission.

ISBN: 978-1647902001
Publisher: Dylanna Publishing, Inc.
First Edition: 2022
10 9 8 7 6 5 4 3 2 1

For information about special discounts for bulk purchases, please contact:

Dylanna Publishing, Inc.
www.dylannapublishing.com

Contents

Meet the Tiger　　6
What Do Tigers Look Like?　　9
Where Do Tigers Live?　　10
Tiger Subspecies　　13
What Do Tigers Eat?　　14
Built to Hunt: Tiger Adaptations　　17
The Hunt　　18
A Day in the Life　　20
Mating and Birth　　23
Growing Up Tiger　　24
Life in the Territory　　27
Lifespan and Population　　28
Predators and Threats　　31
Tigers and Their Ecosystem　　32
Conclusion　　35
Test Your Tiger Knowledge!　　36
STEM Challenge: Think Like a Scientist!　　37
Word Search　　38
Glossary　　39
Resources and References　　40
Index　　41

Meet the Tiger

A shadow moves through the tall grass. Stripes of orange and black blur with golden sunlight filtering through trees. Then—stillness. Somewhere in the Asian jungle, one of nature's most magnificent hunters waits in perfect silence. Welcome to the world of tigers!

Tigers are found across Asia, from snowy Siberian forests to steamy tropical jungles. Tigers once roamed from Turkey to eastern Russia and down to Indonesia. Today, they survive in scattered pockets across 13 countries, with about 70% living in India.

Six **subspecies** of tigers still exist in the wild. The Bengal tiger is most common, making up about 80% of all wild tigers. Their scientific name is *Panthera tigris*—they're related to lions, jaguars, leopards, and cheetahs in the big cat family.

What makes tigers truly special is their **solitary** nature. Unlike lions who live in prides, tigers are lone hunters. Each claims its own territory, silently patrolling through forests and defending it fiercely from rivals. They prefer to stalk and ambush prey in the shadows rather than chase it across open ground.

For thousands of years, tigers have symbolized power, stealth, and wild beauty in cultures across Asia.

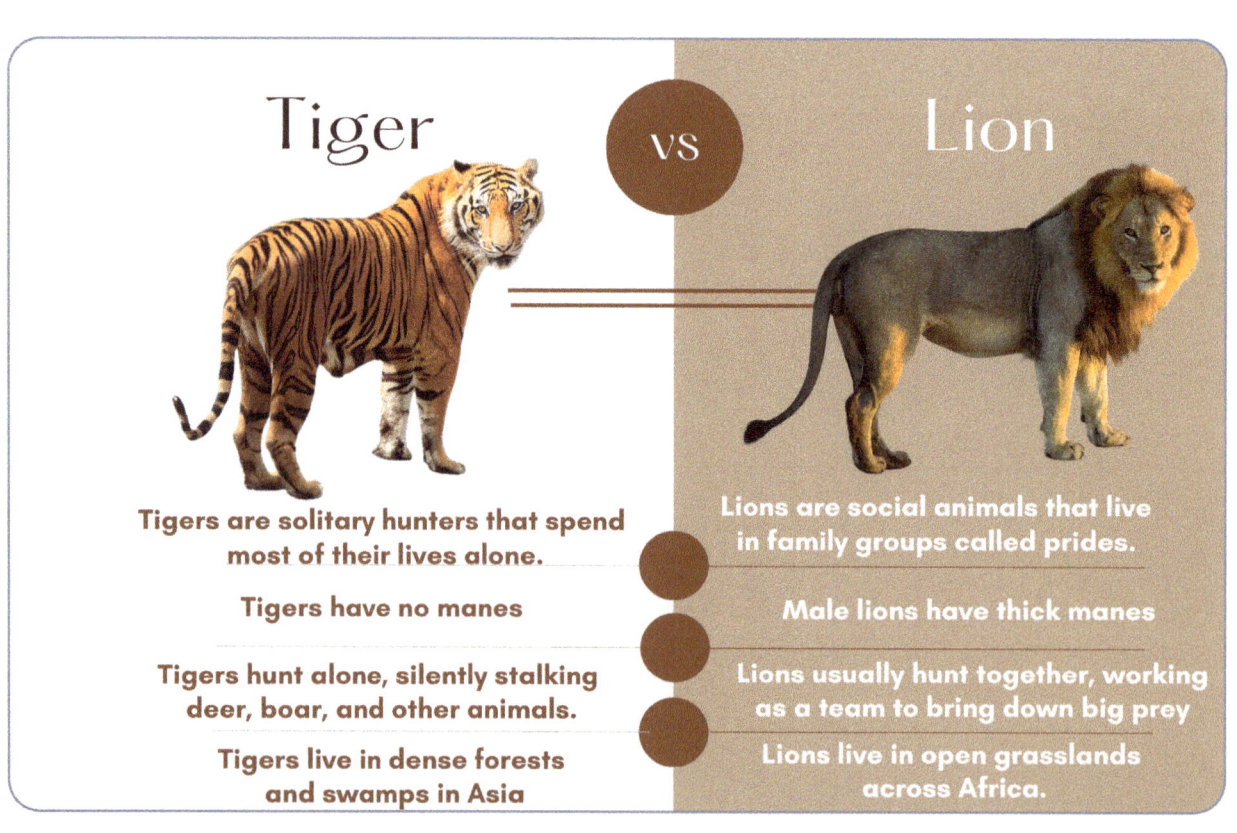

Fun Fact: Tigers can roar, but they rarely do! Unlike lions who roar to communicate across the savanna, tigers prefer to stay silent—sneaking through forests like striped shadows.

Fun Fact: Tigers' stripes go all the way down to their skin! If you shaved a tiger (please don't!), you'd still see the stripe pattern beneath the fur.

What Do Tigers Look Like?

Tigers are BIG—the biggest members of the cat family! Males weigh 220 to 660 pounds (100 to 300 kg)—about the same as three to five adult humans. Females are smaller at 140 to 370 pounds (65 to 170 kg). From nose to tail tip, tigers can stretch 9 to 12 feet (2.7 to 3.7 meters) long. That's longer than most couches!

Their coat is unmistakable: golden orange fur with bold black vertical stripes. No two tigers have the same stripe pattern—each one is unique like a human fingerprint! Some rare tigers are born with white fur, tan stripes, and blue eyes.

Those stripes aren't just beautiful—they're perfect **camouflage.** When a tiger crouches in tall grass or dappled shadows, the black stripes break up its outline. **Prey** animals often look right at a tiger without seeing it!

> **DID YOU KNOW?**
> No two tigers have the same stripe pattern—each one is as unique as a human fingerprint!

Tigers have retractable claws up to 4 inches (10 cm) long and 30 teeth including four canine teeth up to 3 inches (7.6 cm) long—basically daggers designed for grabbing prey. Their massive paws can deliver crushing blows with one swipe.

Here's something amazing: tigers can see in near-total darkness! Their eyes have a special mirror-like layer that bounces light back, making their night vision six times better than ours. This makes their eyes glow green at night—perfect for hunting in shadows!

Where Do Tigers Live?

Tigers live in forests, grasslands, mangrove swamps, and rainforests across Asia. These areas with dense vegetation are perfect for tigers because they can use cover to sneak close to prey.

Tigers survive in amazing diversity—from snowy Siberian forests where temperatures drop below freezing to steamy tropical rainforests. Some even live in mangrove swamps where saltwater meets jungle!

A tiger's territory ranges from 10 to 400 square miles (25 to 1,000 square km), depending on prey availability. Where food is abundant, territories are smaller. In harsh environments, tigers need larger territories to find enough food.

Sadly, 95% of tigers' historical lands have been destroyed by logging, farming, and settlement. Today's tigers live in isolated pockets, making it hard to find mates and maintain healthy populations.

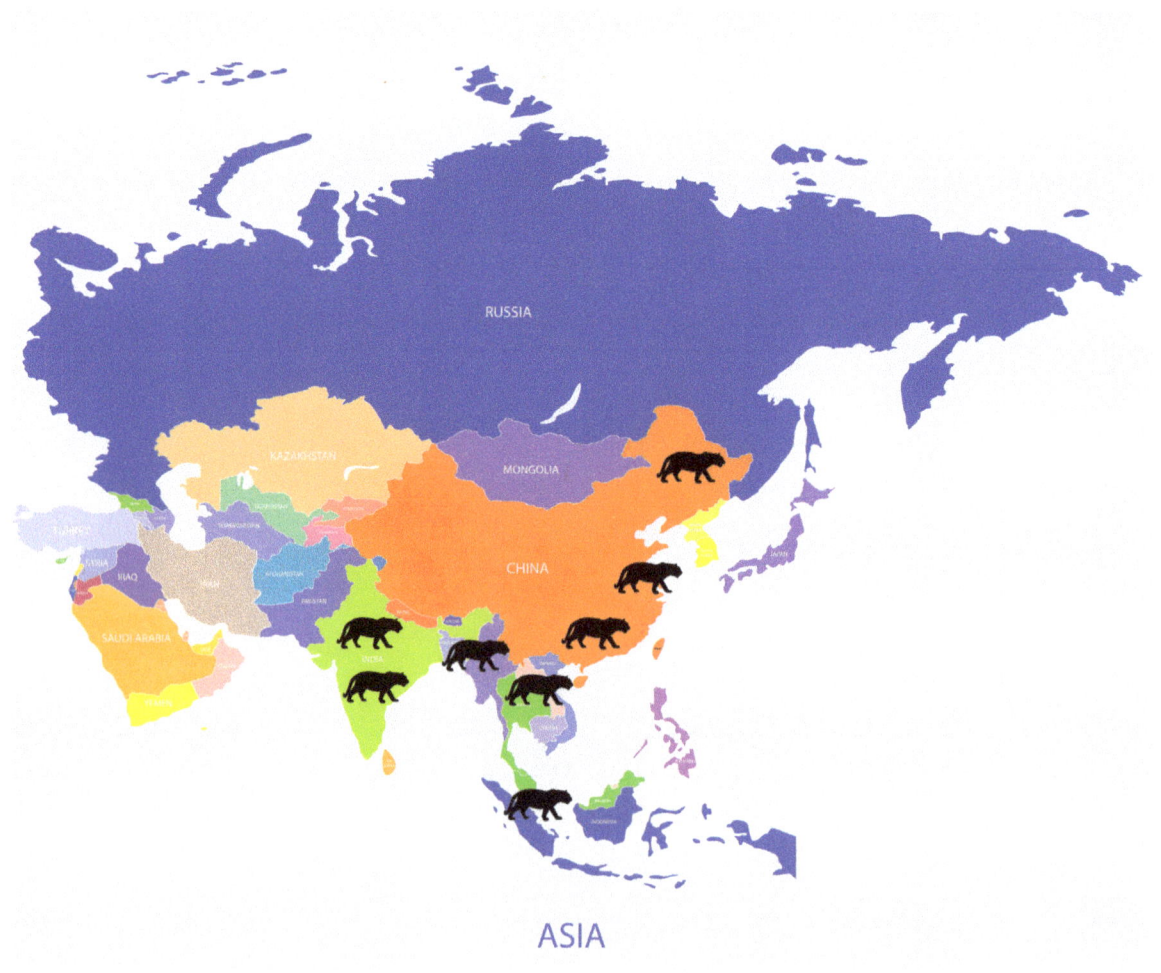

ASIA

Fun Fact: Tigers once ranged across all of Asia and parts of Turkey—but today, they occupy less than 10% of their historic range.

Fun Fact: Tigers are excellent swimmers! Unlike most cats, tigers love water. They wade into rivers to cool off and are strong enough to swim several miles!

Tiger Subspecies

Six types of tigers still roam the wild, each perfectly adapted to its own environment. From icy forests to steamy jungles, these striped cats rule very different worlds!

Subspecies	Where They Live	Population	Special Features
Bengal Tiger (*P. t. tigris*)	India, Bangladesh, Nepal, Bhutan	~3,000	Most common; bright orange coat with narrow stripes
Siberian Tiger (*P. t. altaica*)	Russia, NE China, N. Korea	~500	Largest tiger; thick, pale fur for icy forests
Sumatran Tiger (*P. t. sumatrae*)	Sumatra (Indonesia)	~400	Smallest; darkest stripes for jungle camouflage
Indochinese Tiger (*P. t. corbetti*)	Thailand, Myanmar, Laos, Vietnam, Cambodia	~350	Medium-sized; darker coat and shorter stripes
Malayan Tiger (*P. t. jacksoni*)	Malaysia, southern Thailand	~150	Slightly smaller; critically endangered
South China Tiger (*P. t. amoyensis*)	Southern China (likely extinct in wild)	<10 wild; ~100 captive	Broad, widely spaced stripes; most endangered

Three tiger subspecies—the Bali, Caspian, and Javan tigers—went extinct within the last 80 years. Protecting the remaining six has never been more important!

What Do Tigers Eat?

Tigers are **carnivores**—they eat only meat. They mainly hunt deer, wild boar, water buffalo, and antelope. If larger prey is unavailable, they'll catch fish, frogs, birds, monkeys, and even bears!

A tiger eats 10 to 25 pounds (4.5 to 11 kg) of meat per day. But when they make a kill, they gorge themselves! A tiger can eat up to 100 pounds (45 kg) in one night—about 20% of their body weight!

After such a feast, tigers might not hunt for several days. They typically kill one large animal per week but can go 10 days without eating. They return to their kill repeatedly, guarding it and eating until nothing remains.

Unlike lions, solitary tigers don't have to share! They eat their fill, rest near the carcass, and return when hungry again.

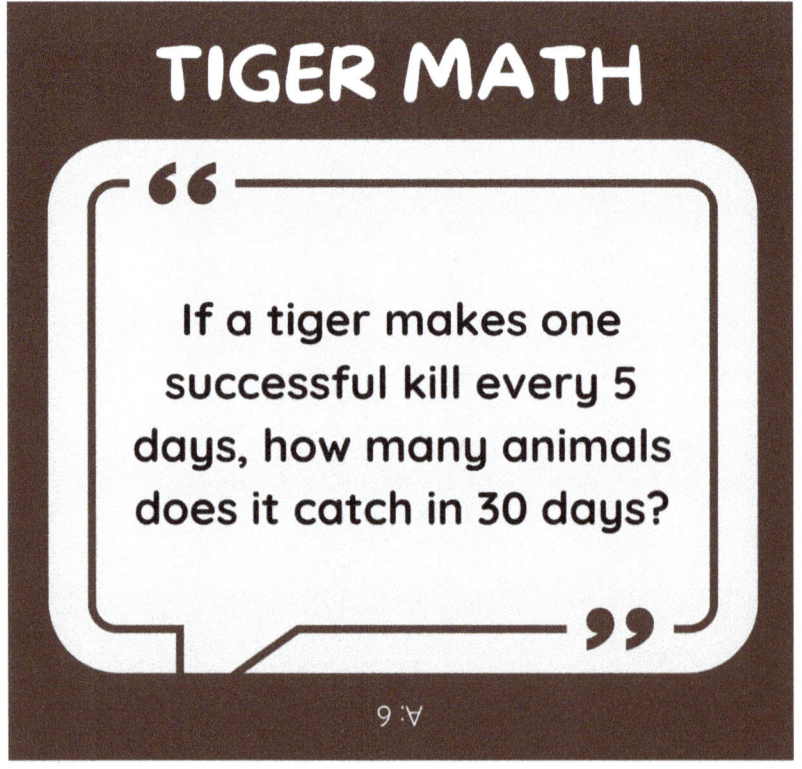

TIGER MATH

"If a tiger makes one successful kill every 5 days, how many animals does it catch in 30 days?"

Fun Fact: A tiger's striped coat helps it blend into tall grass and shadows—making it nearly invisible to its prey.

Built to Hunt: Tiger Adaptations

Tigers are **apex predators**—the rulers of their **ecosystems**. Fully grown, they have no natural enemies, and every part of their body is built for power, stealth, and precision.

Weapons of the Wild

A tiger's body is armed for hunting. Its retractable claws, up to 4 inches (10 cm) long, stay razor-sharp by sheathing inside the paws when not in use. Its canine teeth—about 3 inches (7.5 cm) long—are made to grip and pierce. With jaws strong enough to crush bone and muscular paws capable of breaking a spine in a single swipe, tigers hunt with strength and accuracy.

Super Senses

Tigers rely on extraordinary senses to survive. Their night vision is about six times better than a human's, allowing them to see clearly in near darkness. Ears that swivel in all directions pick up the faintest rustle—sometimes from more than a mile away. Their whiskers act like radar, detecting obstacles or movements in pitch-black conditions. Even their sense of smell helps track prey and mark territory.

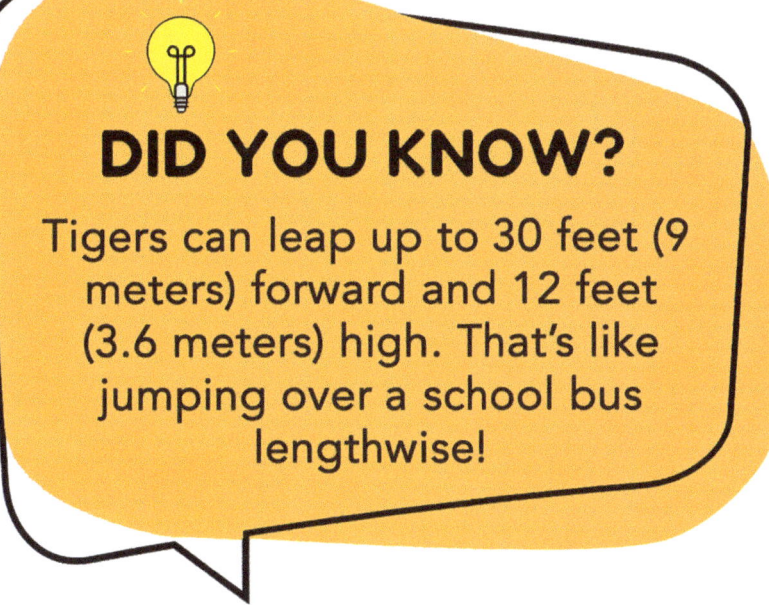

DID YOU KNOW?
Tigers can leap up to 30 feet (9 meters) forward and 12 feet (3.6 meters) high. That's like jumping over a school bus lengthwise!

Perfectly Engineered Hunters

A tiger's orange-and-black stripes act as camouflage, blending into tall grass, trees, and shadowy forests. Padded paws allow them to move silently, while long, muscular tails help with balance during fast turns. And when it's time to strike, tigers can sprint up to 40 mph (65 km/h) for short bursts—fast enough to bring down almost any animal in their path.

From the tips of their whiskers to the ends of their tails, tigers are built for one purpose: to be the ultimate hunters of the wild.

Fun Fact: Tigers are incredibly strong! They can drag prey weighing up to 500 pounds (225 kg) considerable distances—like dragging a full-grown horse through the forest!

The Hunt

Tigers are solitary hunters who typically hunt at night, using darkness and incredible night vision to ambush unsuspecting prey.

A typical hunt follows these steps:

Spotting: Tigers use excellent eyesight and hearing to detect prey, looking for young, old, sick, or injured animals.

Stalking: The tiger creeps forward using every bit of cover—bushes, grass, shadows, trees. It moves incredibly slowly, freezing whenever prey looks its way. This can take 30 minutes or more!

The Rush: When prey is within 30-50 feet (9-15 meters), the tiger explodes from cover at up to 40 mph (65 km/h)! The prey often has no time to react.

The Takedown: Tigers pounce with massive paws to knock prey off balance. Once down, they bite the throat or back of the neck.

Because tigers can't maintain top speed for long, stealth and surprise are crucial. Hunting success rate is only 5-10%—for every kill, a tiger makes 10 to 20 failed attempts!

A Day in the Life

Tigers are most active during twilight—dawn and dusk—when dim light gives them an advantage and prey is moving between feeding areas. They're also comfortable hunting at night when their superior vision helps.

After a successful hunt, tigers drag kills to secluded spots and may cover carcasses with leaves, returning over several days to feed.

By mid-morning, tigers seek shade—under vegetation, in caves, or near water where it's cooler. They sleep 16-20 hours per day, conserving energy between hunts!

DID YOU KNOW?
Tigers use scent marks, scratches on trees, growls, and even facial expressions to communicate with other tigers.

During rest, tigers doze, groom themselves, and often take dips in water.

Unlike most cats, tigers LOVE water! They're strong swimmers who wade into rivers to cool off, play, or even hunt fish.

As evening approaches, tigers patrol territory boundaries, leaving scent marks by spraying urine and scratching tree bark. These marks warn others: "This territory is taken!"

Fun Fact: Tigers sleep in strange positions—sprawled on their backs with legs in the air, draped over rocks, or curled in tight balls!

Fun Fact: Tiger mothers are incredibly patient! Cubs practice "hunting" by pouncing on mom's twitching tail for hours!

Mating and Birth

Tigers live **solitary** lives but come together briefly to mate. Female territories often overlap with one or more male territories. They communicate through scent marking, tree scratches, and vocalizations.

Tigers are **polygamous**—both males and females may have multiple partners. They reach maturity around three to four years old.

When a female is ready to mate, she marks territory frequently and makes special calls. The pair stays together for a few days, then the male leaves and the female raises cubs alone.

After about 100 days of pregnancy, the tigress finds a hidden den in a cave, hollow tree, or dense thicket. She gives birth to two to four cubs, each weighing just 2-4 pounds (1-2 kg). The tiny cubs are born blind and helpless.

NEWBORN CUB STATS
- Birth weight: 2–4 lb (1–2 kg)
- Eyes open: 7–14 days
- Walking: 2–3 weeks
- Weaning: 3–6 months

For the first weeks, the den is a quiet, hidden world. The mother leaves only to hunt, returning to nurse. At around 8 weeks, she begins bringing cubs out to explore.

Growing Up Tiger

Tiger cubs are curious, playful bundles of energy! For the first 8 weeks, they stay hidden in the den. Once their eyes open and they can walk, their real education begins.

Cubs play constantly—wrestling teaches fighting, stalking hones hunting, pouncing develops their spring, and chase games build speed. These games are actually serious survival lessons!

Mother tigers are fiercely protective, fighting to the death against threats like leopards, pythons, wild dogs, and even other male tigers who sometimes kill cubs.

Cubs taste meat around 2-3 months and are weaned by 6 months. At 11 months, they begin trying to hunt themselves—and they're terrible at it! But with each attempt, they improve. By 18 months, they successfully catch smaller prey.

Sadly, 30-40% of cubs don't survive their first two years. Starvation is the biggest threat, along with predators, disease, and injuries.

Female cubs stay with mother until about 2-2.5 years. Males leave earlier, around 18-24 months, becoming nomads who wander searching for unclaimed territory.

MYTH VS FACT

MYTH: Tiger cubs can hunt as soon as they start eating meat.

FACT: Cubs don't master hunting until they're about two years old. They practice by pouncing and stalking during play.

Fun Fact: Tiger cubs go from fast asleep to full-speed running in seconds, wrestle into exhausted heaps, then crash anywhere!

Life in the Territory

Unlike lions, tigers spend most of their lives alone. Adult tigers claim and defend territories, only tolerating others during brief mating periods or when mothers raise cubs.

A tiger's territory provides adequate prey, water, and shelter. Male territories (30-400 square miles) are much larger than female territories (8-60 square miles). A male's territory usually overlaps with two or three females, giving him access to mates.

Tigers patrol constantly, marking boundaries with urine spray, tree scratches, and paw scent. These marks warn: "This territory is occupied!"

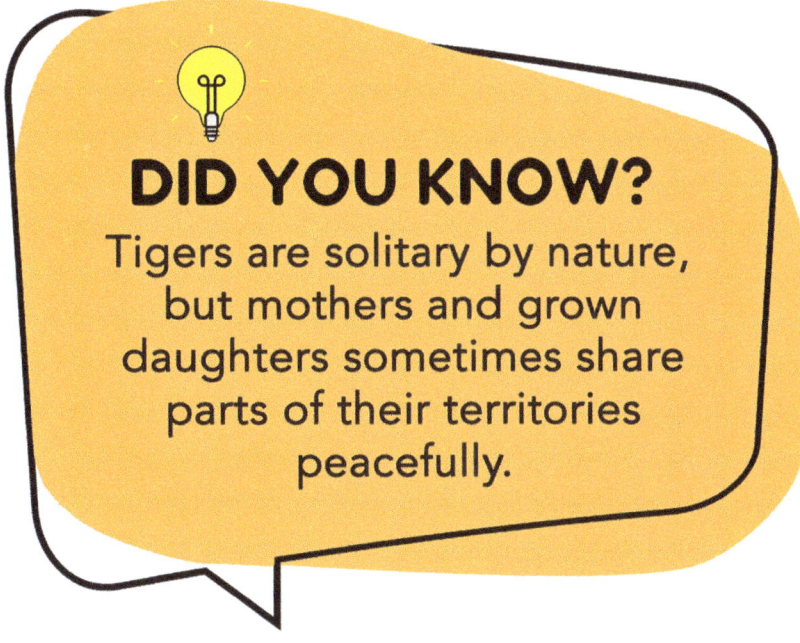

DID YOU KNOW? Tigers are solitary by nature, but mothers and grown daughters sometimes share parts of their territories peacefully.

Communication: Tigers roar, growl, snarl, hiss, chuff, and moan. Their roar travels up to 2 miles (3 km) to warn intruders or call mates. They make friendly "chuffing" sounds—soft snorts—when greeting peacefully. Tree scratches serve as visual markers while keeping claws sharp.

When tigers encounter each other, reactions depend on sex, size, and circumstances. Females with cubs are extremely aggressive. Males fight fiercely over territory. But sometimes tigers tolerate each other—especially during mating season.

Lifespan and Population

In the wild, tigers typically live 8-10 years, though some reach 15 if they avoid injury and starvation. In captivity with guaranteed food and veterinary care, they can live 20-26 years.

Only about 3,900 tigers remain in the wild as of 2024. This is up from 3,200 in 2010 but still represents a 95% decline from an estimated 100,000 tigers a century ago. All six remaining subspecies are endangered.

DID YOU KNOW?
Wild tigers usually live 10–15 years, but in zoos or sanctuaries, some have reached over 25 years old thanks to regular food and medical care.

Most wild tigers live in India (about 3,000), with smaller populations in Russia (500 Siberian tigers), Indonesia (400 Sumatran tigers), and scattered groups in Bangladesh, Bhutan, China, Malaysia, Myanmar, Nepal, and Thailand.

Three subspecies have gone extinct: Bali tiger (1940s), Caspian tiger (1970s), and Javan tiger (1980s).

Tigers have vanished from 93% of their historic range due to habitat loss (farms and cities destroying forests), poaching (illegal hunting for fur and body parts), prey depletion (overhunting of deer and boar), and human-tiger conflict (retaliation when tigers kill livestock).

Despite these challenges, **conservation** programs are helping some populations stabilize and grow!

Fun Fact: India's tiger population has grown from about 1,400 in 2008 to over 3,000 today through dedicated protection!

Fun Fact: Tigers rarely back down from a challenge. They've been known to drive away leopards and packs of wild dogs that enter their territory.

Predators and Threats

Fully grown tigers are apex predators—nothing hunts them in the wild. But their cubs are another story. For young tigers, danger lurks at every turn.

Threats to Cubs

The forest can be a dangerous place for young cubs. Leopards, bears, wild dogs, crocodiles, and even giant pythons will attack if they find cubs unguarded. The greatest danger, however, comes from adult male tigers. When a new male takes over a territory, he often kills cubs that aren't his own to bring the females back into breeding condition. It's harsh, but it's part of nature's cycle.

DID YOU KNOW?
Every part of a tiger's body—skin, bones, teeth, claws—is traded illegally. This cruel demand is one of the biggest reasons tigers are disappearing.

Even without predators, cubs face another deadly threat—hunger. When prey is scarce or a mother is injured, her cubs are the first to go hungry. In the wild, many don't survive their first year.

The Biggest Threat: Humans

While nature is challenging, the most serious danger comes from people. Human activity has caused a 95% decline in tiger numbers over the past century.

Across Asia, forests have been cleared for farming, roads, and cities, destroying more than 90% of tiger habitat. **Poachers** continue to kill tigers for their skins, bones, teeth, and claws, which are sold illegally. At the same time, hunters target the deer and boar tigers rely on for food, leaving the big cats to starve.

As villages and livestock spread deeper into tiger country, human-tiger conflicts have increased. When tigers prey on farm animals, people often retaliate with poison or guns. In coastal regions, climate change adds another threat—rising sea levels and stronger storms are shrinking tiger habitats even further.

Protecting tigers means protecting their forests, their prey, and the people who share their land. When tigers thrive, the entire ecosystem thrives with them.

Tigers and Their Ecosystem

Tigers aren't just magnificent hunters—they're essential to forest health. As apex predators, they maintain balance among all animals in their habitat.

By preying on **herbivores** like deer, wild boar, and water buffalo, tigers prevent any species from becoming too numerous. This keeps forests from being overgrazed, allowing plants to thrive and supporting countless insects, birds, and smaller mammals.

DID YOU KNOW? Forests with healthy tiger populations store huge amounts of carbon, making tiger conservation important for fighting climate change.

When tiger numbers drop, herbivores multiply rapidly, vegetation disappears, and land degrades. Entire ecosystems can unravel without these top predators.

Tigers also influence where prey animals graze, creating a patchwork of heavily and lightly grazed zones that increases biodiversity.

Every tiger kill feeds hundreds of creatures. After tigers eat, leftovers provide food for vultures, jackals, wild dogs, smaller cats, rodents, insects, and soil organisms.

Scientists call tigers "ecosystem engineers"—species whose presence shapes their environment. Protecting tigers means protecting entire ecosystems including forests that clean air and water, prey species, hundreds of other animals, medicinal plants, and watersheds millions of people use.

Fun Fact: In India, tiger reserves protect not just tigers but also Asian elephants, leopards, sloth bears, hundreds of bird species, and thousands of plants!

Conclusion

Tigers are magnificent animals that inspire us with their power, beauty, and mysterious nature. From stunning striped coats to solitary lifestyles, they captivate us in countless ways.

These remarkable cats are ecosystem engineers who shape entire forests. They control herbivore populations, provide food for scavengers, and maintain balance in Asian ecosystems. Without tigers, entire forests would change dramatically.

Tigers have evolved incredible adaptations: camouflage stripes, powerful bodies, sharp weapons, excellent senses, and the patience to stalk prey silently for hours. Their ability to hunt alone in dense forests makes them perfectly suited to life in shadows.

Yet despite their strength, tigers face an uncertain future. Human activities have reduced populations by 95% in just a century. Habitat loss, poaching, prey depletion, and human-tiger conflict threaten their existence.

But there's hope! Conservation programs are making real differences. Protected reserves, anti-poaching patrols, community partnerships, and wildlife corridors are helping populations stabilize and even grow.

Tigers have survived millions of years through countless challenges. They've inspired cultures across Asia for millennia. They've earned their place as symbols of wild beauty and untamed nature.

The question isn't whether we can save tigers—it's whether we will. With commitment and action, we can ensure tigers continue to prowl Asian forests for generations to come.

The striped shadow of the forest needs our help—and the future is in our hands.

Test Your Tiger Knowledge!

Think you remember everything about these magnificent striped cats? Test yourself with these questions!

1. What is a tiger's scientific name?
   A) Felis tigris B) Panthera tigris C) Tigris africanus D) Panthera leo

2. True or False: Tigers love to swim and often cool off in water.

3. How many subspecies of tigers still exist in the wild today?
   A) Three B) Six C) Nine D) Twelve

4. What makes each tiger's stripe pattern special?
   A) All tigers have identical stripes
   B) Stripes change as tigers age
   C) Each tiger's pattern is unique like a fingerprint
   D) Only males have stripes

5. Where do most of the world's wild tigers live today?
   A) China B) Russia C) India D) Indonesia

6. What is the main purpose of a tiger's stripes?
   A) To attract mates B) Camouflage in grass and shadows C) To scare prey
   D) To regulate body temperature

7. How many hours per day do tigers typically sleep or rest?
   A) 8-10 hours B) 12-14 hours C) 16-20 hours D) 22-24 hours

8. What is the biggest threat to tiger survival today?
   A) Natural predators B) Disease C) Human activities (habitat loss and poaching) D) Climate only

9. 9. Approximately how many wild tigers remain in the world today?
   A) 1,000 B) 3,900 C) 50,000 D) 100,000

10. What is a tiger's conservation status according to the IUCN?
    A) Least Concern B) Vulnerable C) Endangered D) Critically Endangered

Answer Key: 1-B, 2-True, 3-B, 4-C, 5-C, 6-B, 7-C, 8-C, 9-B, 10-C

STEM Challenge: Think Like a Scientist!

Lions are built for power and teamwork. Try these hands-on experiments to discover how their adaptations help them survive!

Camouflage Test

Topic: Animal Adaptation

You'll Need:
Construction paper (orange, black, yellow, green, brown), scissors, timer, grassy or forested area (or indoor space with varied background)

What to Do:

1. Cut identical lion shapes from each color
2. Have a helper hide them in grass while you close your eyes
3. Set a timer for 2 minutes and find as many as you can
4. Which colors were hardest to find?

What You'll Learn:
Tigers' orange-and-black striped fur helps them blend into dappled forest shadows and golden grasslands, making them nearly invisible to prey!

Stalking Challenge

Topic: Patience and Stealth

You'll Need:
Blindfold, small bell or jingly object, open space

What to Do:

1. One person wears the blindfold and holds the bell (they're the "prey")
2. Another person tries to sneak up and tag them without making the bell jingle (they're the "tiger")
3. The "prey" listens carefully and points when they hear something
4. Take turns—who's the stealthiest stalker?

What You'll Learn:
Tigers must move incredibly slowly and silently to get close enough to pounce. Patience and stealth are more important than speed!

 # Word Search

```
T R S F O O D C H A I N P E Z
E A R I Q X K C L Y V W D L G
R N O X C R Q J H S U B M A E
R G T A D A P T A T I O N S G
I E A C O N S E R V A T I O N
T N D X S E R O V I N R A C L
O O E K S E I C E P S B U S H
R I R V H A B I T A T S X X Q
I T P B B E N D A N G E R E D
A A Y L I M A F E A D I L E F
L Z L N O C T U R N A L J Z P
S I A N A P S E F I L E M A O
R L V S E N S E S A H C R W A
E A I T E G A L F U O M A C C
G C V Z Z G I H N N Z R S E H
I O R R V K H O I C R C J B I
T V U J L O Q A C V H R H R N
G D S Y R A T I L O S Y A B G
```

ADAPTATIONS   FOOD CHAIN   SENSES
AMBUSH   HABITATS   SOLITARY
CAMOUFLAGE   LIFESPAN   SUBSPECIES
CARNIVORES   NOCTURNAL   SURVIVAL
CONSERVATION   POACHING   TERRITORIAL
ENDANGERED   PREDATORS   TIGERS
FELIDAE FAMILY RANGE   VOCALIZATION

Glossary

adaptations – special features or behaviors that help a plant or animal survive in its environment

ambush – a surprise attack from a concealed or hidden position

apex predator – an animal at the top of the food chain with no natural predators when healthy and adult

camouflage – coloring or patterns that help an animal blend in with its surroundings to hide from predators or prey

carnivore – an animal that eats only meat

conservation – protecting natural resources, habitats, and wildlife for future generations

ecosystem – all the living things and their environment in a particular area, and how they interact

habitat – the natural home or environment where a plant or animal lives

herbivore – an animal that eats only plants

poaching – the illegal killing and trafficking of wild animals

polygamous – having more than one mate; both male and female lions mate with multiple partners

prey – an animal that is hunted by another animal for food

solitary – living or existing alone

subspecies – a subdivision of a species; groups within the same species that have slight differences

territory – an area of land that an animal or group defends as their own

Resources and References

Want to learn more about tigers and Asian wildlife? Check out these trusted books, websites, and organizations dedicated to understanding and protecting these magnificent big cats.

Books
Tigers by Valmik Thapar (Reaktion Books) — Stunning photography and comprehensive information about tiger biology and conservation.

The Tiger: A True Story of Vengeance and Survival by John Vaillant (Knopf) — A gripping account of human-tiger conflict in Russia's Far East.

Tigers of the World: The Science, Politics and Conservation of Panthera tigris edited by Ronald Tilson and Philip J. Nyhus (Academic Press) — Detailed scientific research on all tiger subspecies.

Wild Cats of the World by Luke Hunter and Priscilla Barrett (Princeton University Press) — Comprehensive guide to all wild cat species, including detailed tiger information.

Websites
National Geographic Kids – Tiger Facts
kids.nationalgeographic.com/animals/mammals/facts/tiger
Fun facts, videos, and photos perfect for young readers learning about tigers.

World Wildlife Fund (WWF) – Tiger Conservation
www.worldwildlife.org/species/tiger
Global efforts to protect tigers, their habitat, and prey species.

Panthera – Tiger Program
www.panthera.org/cat/tiger
Leading wild cat conservation organization's tiger protection programs.

Wildlife Conservation Society (WCS) – Tigers
www.wcs.org/species/tiger
Research and conservation programs protecting tigers across Asia.

For Young Scientists
Smithsonian National Zoo – Tigers
nationalzoo.si.edu/animals/tiger
Information about tigers, including live webcams and educational resources.

San Diego Zoo Wildlife Alliance – Tiger
animals.sandiegozoo.org/animals/tiger
Detailed information, videos, and conservation stories about tigers and their relatives.

Global Tiger Forum
www.globaltigerforum.org
International alliance of tiger range countries working to protect wild tigers.

Keep Exploring!

If you enjoyed learning about tigers, explore other titles in the *This Incredible Planet* series to discover more amazing animals—from sea turtles to penguins to elephants—and the habitats they call home.

INDEX

A
adaptations, 17
apex predators, 17
appearance, 9
Asia, 6, 10

B
Bali tiger, 13, 28
Bengal tiger, 6, 13
big cats, 6

C
camouflage, 9, 17
carnivores, 14
Caspian tiger, 13, 28
characteristics, 6, 9
claws, 9, 17
climate change, 32
coat, 9, 17
communication, 27
conservation, 28, 35
cubs, 23, 24–25, 31

D
diet, 14

E
ecosystems, 17, 32
eyes, 9, 18

F
females, 9, 23, 24, 27
fur, 9, 17

H
habitat, 6, 10, 32
hearing, 17
herbivores, 32
humans, 31
hunting, 14, 17, 18–19, 20

I
Indochinese tiger, 13

J
Javan tiger, 13, 28

L
lifespan, 28
lions, 6

M
Malayan tiger, 13

males, 9, 23, 27
mating, 23

N
night vision, 9, 17

P
paws, 9, 17
physical characteristics, 9
poaching, 31
population, 28, 29
predators, 31
pregnancy, 23
prey, 9, 14, 32

R
roaring, 7

S
scent marks, 20, 26
sene, 9
senses, 17
Siberian tiger, 13
size, 9
sleep, 20
smell, 17
South China tiger, 13
stripes, 8, 9, 17
subspecies, 6, 13, 28
Sumatran tiger, 13
swimming, 12, 20

T
teeth, 9, 17
territory, 6, 10, 23, 27
threats, 31

V
vision, 9, 17, 18